Dancing With Father

Michele Okimura

Illustrated by Danielle Iranon

XULON PRESS

Dancing With Father
by Michele Okimura

Printed in the United States of America

ISBN 9781613792711

Unless otherwise indicated, Bible quotations are taken from The Holy Bible, Open Bible edition (KJV). Copyright © 1975 by Thomas Nelson Inc.; and The Holy Bible (NIV). Copyright © 1973, 1978,1984 by International Bible Society.

www.xulonpress.com

Dedicated to all the girls and women
around the world
who have yet to experience the
Father heart of God.

All proceeds from this book will be donated
to Christian ministries that rescue, heal, and
restore victims of human trafficking,
introducing them to the Father.

PRAISE FOR
DANCING WITH FATHER

M ichele's poem prophetically testifies how God the Father was able to unveil Himself to a broken, hurting woman and breathe life, hope and destiny into her. It is a poem that displays the depths of the Father's love for those who feel outcast, wounded, lonely and afraid. By reading this poem, you will be inspired to entrust your heart to Him who is able to change your name and therefore your life!

Rob Gross
Senior Pastor, Mountain View Community Church

Your poem captures how your wounding became a sort of operating theatre into which the Lord entered in order to bring His healing touch. You convey that what He did is larger than you by gesturing to the fact that this is the healing He has for all of His children. You convey both that your healing was wonderful and touching, and that it's not simply a memorial to you: it's also a sign of hope for what He longs to do for us all. Thanks Michele, for sharing your heart with us.

Andy Comiskey
Founder, Desert Stream Ministries

As a friend of Michele's for many years I stand in awe of His amazing grace that permeates all aspects of her life. She fills my heart with deep encouragement, joy-filled laughter, heart-felt prayer, and unconditional love. She has humbly allowed her own woundedness to become a source of hope and life for others. Indeed, she has become what Henri Nouwen calls, "the wounded healer." I love her for that, and know that those who read this poem will too.

Dyne Peich, M.A. Counseling Psychology
Streams of Hope Counseling Services, LLC

Dancing with Father is a prophetic poem that speaks to the spirit of every woman who longs for unconditional love and affirmation. It beautifully captures the process of transformation that can only come through experiencing the kind of unconditional and adoring love that our Father has for all who would respond to his invitation to dance with Him. Indeed, those who know the affirming embrace of the Father are compelled to share it with others...May all who read this poem not only hear the Father's invitation, but like Michele, dare to waltz with Him into deeper experiences of His love.

Dr. Lisa Orimoto, Ph.D.
Clinical Psychologist

During our annual church retreat, I was able to share about some aspects of the way I believe the Lord Jesus Christ views women as feminine beings and how our femininity has been twisted and distorted through time and cultural influences. Near the end of that time, I read *Dancing with Father* from the podium, and The Lord ministered to the women through your words. I believe it also spoke hope and encouragement to many for whom The Lord's gentle inner healing was a new and powerful experience. May the Lord bless this wondrous work for His kingdom purposes, to bring more hurting souls into His love and light, and to turn wayward hearts back to Him!

Lori Kodama
Prayer Ministry Leader, Evergreen Baptist Church, San Gabriel Valley, CA

FORWARD

When I read *Dancing with Father,* I felt moved and touched at a deep and profound level. I found it difficult to put my feelings into words. To describe it means losing something in the translation.

Dancing with Father takes you from the pain of an alone, sad, doubtful little girl who struggles through her pain of rejection and finds love in her Heavenly Father's arms. Michele is able to fully describe her dance with God and all that leads up to it in an easy to read and understandable fashion.

What I found, which was truly inspirational, is how Michele depicted her personal doubt and hesitancy, yet had the courage to take a risk to reach out and hold onto God. The poem teaches us that God is not concerned about our doubt, but that in our doubt, we come to Him and surrender ourselves to Him so that He can show us in His mysterious and almost magical way, that simply saying "Yes" to Him can have a deep and complete cleansing of our soul. In addition, the story teaches us that our purpose is to reach out to others and help bring them to Him so that they can experience His love and healing.

As a therapist, I have used this poem as a healing tool for many women, because it is everyone's story of pain and triumph, or the hope of triumph. Her poem is able to teach, touch, and heal in a way that simply talking and therapeutic techniques could never do. I thank Michele for having the insight and courage to put her experience into words. She not only helped me, but I am sure this poem has helped many others. Michele's openness, sensitivity, and courage to express her life's journey truly touched my heart and those that have heard this poem.

Memrey Casey, LCSW
Director and Co-founder of In His House Hawaii

INTRODUCTION

I remember the incident as if it happened just yesterday. There I was, adorned in a beautiful white gown that mom had sewn for my Senior Prom. Like any typical teenage girl thrilled to be all dressed up and made up for such a distinctive occasion, I stood waiting in our living room with eager anticipation for my date to arrive. Feeling such joy and delight, the words came rolling off my tongue, "How do I look?"

The abrupt response hit me, taking my breath away as I gasped for air. "You look funny" instantly shot back at me in a critical and angry stare. The harsh retort only reinforced the message I had been receiving for years and what I already had come to believe about myself. That brief scene became a defining moment for me because in its brevity, it described a reality I lived in.

Sixteen years later, my husband and I attended a wonderful, week-long Christian conference that taught us how to facilitate God's healing to wounded souls. During lunch on the last day of the conference, the painful memory of my Senior Prom night came back to me. It caught me by surprise because I hadn't thought about the incident for a long time.

After lunch, we met in our assigned small groups as we had every day of the conference. Since this was our last meeting together, we took turns being prayed for by the rest of the group. I didn't tell them about the memory of my senior prom night, but as they prayed, one woman said she immediately had a vision of me in a white dress. Then another woman said that she also immediately saw a vision of me in a white dress while at a dance. A third woman excitedly shared that she too had a vision of me in a white dress, and that Father God wanted to dance with me.

Needless to say, I wept as I heard the Lord speak healing words to my heart regarding this painful memory. This was His new, defining moment for me.

Shortly after that wondrous encounter with Him, I was inspired to write *Dancing with Father*. The poem is a vision of my dance with Father God and a tribute to Him that testifies of how He healed me and gave me a new identity. My hope and prayer is that you also will be drawn into a personal encounter with Father God as you hear Him speak His transforming love to you.

All glory to Him who imparts a crown of beauty instead of ashes, the oil of joy instead of mourning and the garment of praise instead of a spirit of despair!

"...for it is your Father's good pleasure

to give you the kingdom."

(KJV) Luke 12:32

Invited I was
to this dance, this event,
unbelievable to me
an invitation was sent!

My dress was all white
with a delicate flow.
Lace, ribbons and pearls,
silk, satin aglow.

As I peered through the door,
the joy I did see,
on the faces of all
a look relaxed and so free.

A song called me forth
to this glorious place.
I slowly inched in
with a hesitant pace.

The room was alive!
Looking over the scene,
such a chattering crowd,
against the wall I did lean.

Much rejection I knew,
for years I did hide.
Alone and unloved.
Quite ugly inside.

Raging within
heart of turbulent seas.
Not good enough.
Always striving to please.

So in the back row,
I hunched quietly there.
Blended in well.
Did anyone care?

Then above all the music
a gentle word came.
Someone calling for me?
Was it really my name?

Who could it be?
It was Father God's call.
Disbelief at first,
then hope rising tall.

The people near me
were clearing away,
Till I saw Him there,
not a word did I say.

"Could I have this dance?"
He asked me with glee.
"Who me?"
"Yes, you."
Tender eyes fixed on me.

Who am I to be picked?
The struggle began.
The thought then occurred,
"Maybe I can."

"But I feel so unsure,"
I wanted now to retort.
Little did I know
His arms would support.

But what if I stumble?
What if I trip?
So awkward I felt,
would I fall from His grip?

Echoing in my head
loud and clear,
aching pain so familiar,
it often would sear.

Does heaven hear
my lament and my cries?
Rescue me Lord.
Will your eagle's wings rise?

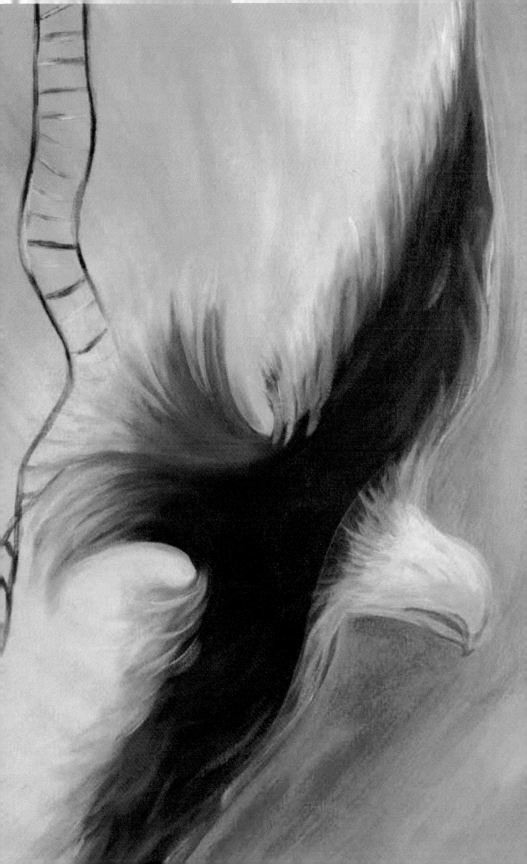

Childhood memories
began swirling in me.
Tormenting words.
Lord, how to be free?

Thought patterns and labels,
in my head loudly rang.
Deep down in my being,
I felt a sharp pang.

Bitterness, despair,
wedged deep in my soul.
Receiving the lies
had taken its toll.

"A Sad Disappointment.
You're not worth very much!"
Shame, fear controlled me,
then I felt His touch.

He placed His two hands
on my head as He spoke.
Declaring out loud,
breaking chains and my yoke.

"You are my daughter!
You're adopted, you're mine.
An orphan no more!
You are part of my vine.

You're worth pursuing,
I'm setting you free.
I'm restoring your heart.
In my presence, just be.

With my help and power,
you can forgive.
You have my Spirit,
walk with me and live!

So take in my smile,
my joy and my peace.
Rest secure in my love,
do trust me, release!"

His hand reached for mine
while the music played on.
It was as we danced,
that the battle was won.

Such compassion I felt,
as never before.
The healing began.
First little, then more.

He asked me a question.
I then lent my ear.
When I heard His voice,
I started to tear.

"For the rest of your life,
could I have this dance?
Will you be my partner?"
Joy inside me did prance.

"When we're together,
you'll see truth and light."
"Yes, Lord," I said,
"With my soul, strength and might.

I'll follow you, Lord,
I'll follow your lead,
though my faith be as small
as a mustard seed."

My shriveled heart
was awakened in me.
Once death, now there's life!
No longer I'll flee.

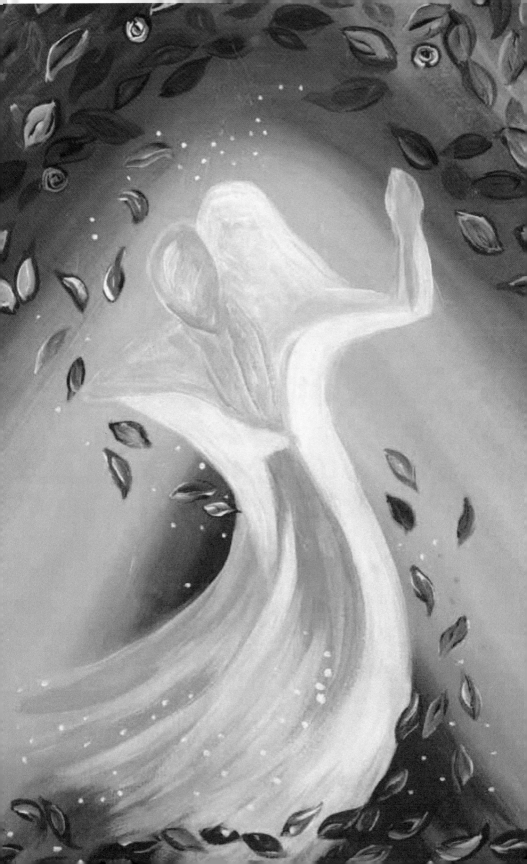

He named me anew,
'Precious Gift Among Saints,'
'Set Apart,' and 'Chosen,'
'A Masterpiece He Paints.'

'Sweet Aroma,' and 'Favored,'
to His arms I will dash.
His awesome power
made beauty from ash.

Such unspeakable love,
so wide, deep, and high!
Eternal, transforming.
He answered my cry.

My eyes were then drawn
to my dress pure and white.
This He provided.
Such beauty, so bright!

Then a vision appeared
of His passionate love.
So kind and unending,
as gentle as a dove.

These scenes from my Lord
hide in me everyday,
through this He is teaching me
His holy way.

I was in a large room
with some women there too.
I was dressing them in
gowns of white hue.

Then to others 'round them,
they did likewise.
Now sensitive women,
they could hear silent cries.

The comfort received
must be given away.
May all know His love,
I now earnestly pray.

He gave me a purpose,
a mission of sorts,
to prepare those that seek Him
to adorn His bright courts.

To help other daughters
get dressed pretty and fair,
for inside and out,
they're exquisitely rare!

To help clothe them in truth
of who they now are.
Each princess crowned,
a shining, bright star.

To help ready them for
a time ever so true,
for the dance of their lives
that would make them brand new.

And so I received
His blessing and call.
This dance with The Father
had broken my wall.

The miracle of change
He has done deep in me,
has opened my eyes,
once blind, now I see.

As I journey with Him,
it is Him I pursue.
To Him all honor,
praise, glory is due!

'Dancing With Father.'
Do you hear His song?
Please come right on in,
He's been waiting so long.

A bright future awaits,
He offers you hope.
More than survive.
More than just cope.

Hear Father's love song,
His voice beckoning now.
Let Him lead you in faith,
He will show you how.

You'll be safe in His arms,
in His warm embrace.
He'll keep you in step
to His rhythm and pace.

What joy waits for you
if you answer God's call.
Would you dear beloved,
come to The King's ball?

Support the Fight
Against Human Trafficking

"Defend the cause of the weak and fatherless;
Maintain the rights of the poor and oppressed.
Rescue the weak and needy;
Deliver them from the hand of the wicked.
Psalm 82:3-4 NIV

Human trafficking is estimated to be a $32 billion industry, one of the biggest and fastest growing criminal activities in the world today. More than two million people a year are coerced and sold into slavery for forced labor and sexual exploitation, with an estimated 50% of them being children.

All profits made from the sale of this book will be donated to Christian ministries that are actively bringing justice, salvation, hope and healing of Jesus Christ to children and young women in Southeast Asia who are in serious danger of being sold into slavery or they have already been victimized.

About the Author

MICHELE OKIMURA and her husband Rob are founding pastors of Hope Chapel Lifespring in Honolulu, Hawaii. A devoted wife and mother of two children who understands the challenges facing families today, she also is the founder and director of Kingdom Families Hawaii, a ministry that creates venues for strengthening families and raising children to be passionate followers of Jesus Christ.

Knowing from personal experience the power of God to heal and transform broken lives, Michele's passion is to see people of all ages deeply encounter the Father and His love so that they are free to walk in their true identity and bring glory to Him.

CPSIA information can be obtained
at www.ICGtesting.com
Printed in the USA
239948LV00001B